Nottinghai
Post Off

on old picture p

David Ottewell

A standard postcard design with overprint of Southwell. Different place-names would be included to suit the point of sale. This was a mailing novelty, with miniature views of Southwell enclosed in the postman's bag. The card was posted from the town in August 1913.

£3.50

Introduction

At the beginning of the twentieth century, most villages in Nottinghamshire had their own post office. Even in this period of horse-drawn delivery carts, these post offices received two deliveries of mail each weekday. Sadly, a hundred years later, the number of village and suburban post offices is rapidly declining and people are having to travel increasing distances to access postal services. With the abolition of the so-called second delivery (a luxury that most of us haven't enjoyed for many years!) the delivery of mail in this technological age has actually got worse.

Researching this book, it was interesting to note the number of sub postmasters and mistresses who served for 30 years and longer. Often they would then pass the position onto another member of the family. Obviously, if the post office was in part of the family home, this was a natural course of events. Conversely, in some villages the post office was regularly on the move. In my own small village, the post office has had six different homes over the years.

Frequently the sub postmaster/mistress would combine the post office with another business; most commonly this would be a grocery or newsagents. But in some cases, less usual lines would be offered alongside the postal services. These ranged from bicycles and watches to clothes and photographic equipment. One post office was in a bakers; another a chemists. A further one housed a library.

Hopefully, a look through this book will arouse feelings of nostalgia for when you could go into your local post office and receive personal service. If you still can, maybe you will appreciate how lucky you are.

Over the twentieth century, a large number of publishers produced postcards featuring views of village post offices. Obviously this was shrewd business practice on their part, for the post office would sell the cards for use by their customers.

Picture postcards were first published in Britain in 1894, but it was not until a decade later that they began to take off, when in 1902, the Post Office allowed a message to be written on the address side. This meant that the whole of one side was available for the picture and this gave more scope to the publisher. Photographic viewcards became very popular and the postcard became the most important way of communicating news or messages, in much the same way as the telephone or emails are used today. The years up to 1914 were the *Golden Age* of picture postcards, when millions of imaginative designs covering every subject under the sun were published by a host of national and local firms. Where known, postcard publishers have been acknowledged.

Anyone wanting further information on the history of the post offices in their locality should visit Nottingham Local Studies Library and ask to see Dennis Humphrey's 10-volume *Nottingham Postal History* - a comprehensive and invaluable piece of research.

David Ottewell
August 2004

Front cover: it must have taken some organisation to assemble all the staff outside Mansfield's main post office for local photographer JW Sylvester of Woodhouse Road to take this picture. The clock tells us it was 6.40 but there is no indication of date.

Back cover (top): At the beginning of the twentieth century, Ernest Robert Bembridge was sub postmaster at his shop 2 Central Avenue, Bridgford Road in West Bridgford, where he also sold groceries and was a beer, wines and spirits merchant.

(bottom): see illustration 8 for caption.

1. Henry George Owston of **Annesley Woodhouse** published a number of postcards of the area, including this one of his own shop. In addition to operating the post office from 1901 to 1949, he also traded as a draper, clothier and grocer.

2. With a population of 372 in 1904, **Aslockton** couldn't have been too complicated a challenge for postmaster George Stevens. The anonymous photographer has organised him, Mrs Stevens and a selection of villagers to pose for this postcard.

3. A schoolboy peering longingly through the window of **Balderton** post office where William Walls acted as sub postmaster from 1912-42. He must have been kept busy, as by 1921 the population of the village had reached 3,132. This postcard is one of a series on Balderton by Lilywhite Ltd of Halifax.

4. Doncaster publisher EL Scrivens produced this postcard showing **Barnby Moor** post office. John Kitchen served as sub postmaster for 43 years from 1912-55. Post arrived daily via Retford. Note the policeman on the opposite side of the road keeping an eye on proceedings.

5. Postally used in **Beeston** in 1918, this 'Clumber' series postcard (no. 431) shows the small single-storey post office building which was opened in 1862. Prior to the First World War, there were three deliveries of mail from Nottingham each day. The building was replaced by a larger post office on the corner of Foster Avenue in 1935.

6. Postally used in 1915, when Miss Florence Bowness was the sub postmistress, this picture shows **Blyth** post office, which was also listed as a 'Public Telephone Call and Telephonic Express Delivery Office'.

7. In 1905, when this postcard was sent, Highbury Road was already a flourishing thoroughfare leading from **Bulwell** to Nottingham (note the tramlines along which a regular service ran linking the two places). At this time, William Ellis, confectioner and tobacconist, also operated the post office. The post box on the shop wall was emptied five times a day.

8. During the Edwardian period, a horse-drawn mail cart brought mail from Nottingham to **Burton Joyce** at 5.50am and 2.30pm, and mail was sent back at 7.10pm. Note the three postmen by the post office which was run from 1904-39 by Ellen Sophie Johnson.

9. During the period 1893-1906, the post office in the village of **Calverton** was run by William Collyer. The photographer has gathered a selection of locals to pose for his picture.

10. At the end of the 1960s, **Calverton** post office was housed in much more up-to-date premises on Crookdale Lane.

11. The building seen here housing **Caunton** post office has served this purpose on four different occasions. This postcard, by Leicester publisher AW Bourne, was published in the 1950s. The car of the period and the *'stop me and buy one'* ice cream cart add interest to the scene.

12. This impressive building served as **Collingham** post office from 1912-1967. During its first 16 years of operation, Annie Gibson is recorded as acting as sub postmistress.

13. This postcard of **Colston Bassett** post office demonstrates the care needed when trying to date pictures. The postcard was postally used in 1934. However, the shop sign shows John Arthur Newton as postmaster. According to records, he retired in 1932. This must have been an old card when sent, as Ernest Frederick Kirchin held the post of sub postmaster from 1932-1962.

14. The centre of the village of **Cotgrave** with the *Manvers Arms* prominent. Opposite stands Walter White's grocers shop. Here for 54 years from 1900-1954, he also acted as village sub postmaster.

15. William Herry Wightman was sub postmaster at 37 Station Street, **East Kirkby**, from 1896-1915. The shop signs suggest he offered many other services from optician to selling watches, jewellery and bicycles.

16. A picture taken from the *Nags Head* on Main Street, **East Leake**, towards the post office. James Arthur Clark began as sub postmaster in this building in 1930. The business stayed in the family, passing to son and then grand-daughter until 1987.

17. A crowd gathered outside the post office in the small village of **Edingley** in 1913 when Mrs MK Beet was sub postmistress. Could that be her standing in the doorway? The post office offered only the basic facilities; people had to travel to Farnsfield for a money order or telegraph office.

18. The village of **Elston**, five miles from Newark, was served by the same sub postmistress for 36 years. From 1928-64, Mrs Eliza Pricilla Spinks carried out this role from the small semi-detatched cottage seen in the distance.

19. A postcard from the Nottingham firm of C & AG Lewis showing **Epperstone** post office in the 1920s. The village's population in 1904 was just 362, with many of them working at the local paper mill.

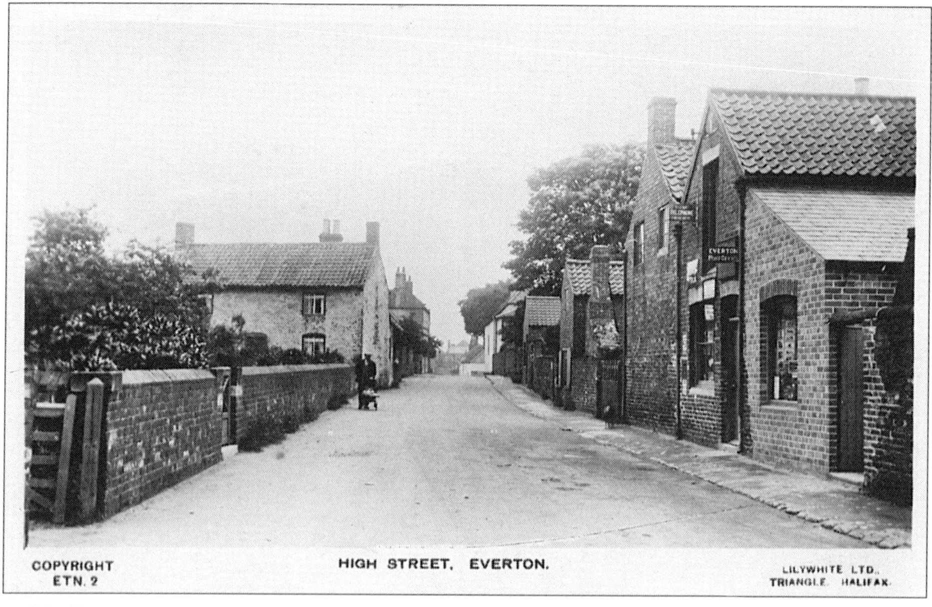

COPYRIGHT
ETN. 2
HIGH STREET, EVERTON.
LILYWHITE LTD.
TRIANGLE HALIFAX

20. Everton, in the north of Nottinghamshire, received its mail via Doncaster. The postcard by Lilywhites of Halifax probably dates from the end of the 1920s when Arther Ellis Gray held the dual role of village baker and sub postmaster. It is interesting to see in the nearest window a display of postcards for sale.

21. ME Summers took this photograph of **Farndon** post office. The postcard was sent in 1932, the year Albert Stanley Foster began a 26-year stint as sub postmaster of the village. Letters arrived from Newark, the nearest large town, for local distribution.

Farndon Green.
Wollaton Park. Nottingham
Rex Photo. 3612

22. Farndon Green was part of an area of houses built on land released by the sale of much of the Wollaton Hall estate in the 1920s. The post office catered for the needs of the residents of the new estate, also acting as a newsagent and confectioner. Card no. 3612 in the 'Rex' series.

23. The Doncaster Rotophoto Company published a number of postcards of the village of **Farnsfield,** including this one of the post office. Mrs Evelyn B Pidcock was sub postmistress in this building for 34 years until 1946 when the post office was transferred to Main Street.

24. As the twentieth century began, **Gonalston** only had a population of 128, but it still had its own post office and received two deliveries of mail a day from Nottingham. Housed in Manor Cottage, it was run from 1898-1930 by the Estate foreman, William Challand Hutchinson.

25. Seven miles from Nottingham, **Gotham** had a population of 1,066 in 1921. This building seems quite small to cater for so many, but it served as the village post office from 1922-38. At this time, Frederick W Kemp was postmaster as well as a confectioner, stationer, tobacconist and photographic materials dealer.

26. The Carnall family ran the post office at 30 Rectory Lane in the village of **Gamston,** North Notts, for 73 years beginning with George Carnall in 1901. Hannah Carnall, who took over as sub postmistress in 1916, published this card herself for sale in the shop.

27. The white building in the distance served as the village post office in the riverside village of **Gunthorpe** from 1929-88. Harold Spouge was sub postmaster from 1932-54 before being succeeded by his son, Robert, who carried out the role for 33 years. Although purchased in 1965, the card dates from some years earlier.

28. Things have changed since this AW Bourne-published card was sent from **Halam** in 1969. The far pub, *The Plough*, has been converted into a private house and the post office no longer exists; it moved to different premises in 1983, but at the time of writing, the village no longer has a post office.

29. The clock above the door of **Hoveringham** post office helps to date the postcard, for this was installed in 1913 when John Thomas Berry was sub postmaster. He was succeeded by George Metcalf Gelsthorpe in 1920 and he went on to hold the post for 30 years. Note the boy on the tricycle.

30. At 106 **Goldsmith Street** in **Nottingham**, John Banks ran a post office and grocer's shop. It is interesting to note that in 1908 the postbox was emptied eleven times each weekday, the first collection being 5am and the last 10.45pm. Oh for such service today!

31. These premises at 18 Main Street served as the post office in **Keyworth**, six miles from Nottingham, from 1937-72. Operations were then transferred to a single-storey building next door. Posted in 1957, the message reads *"Just another card to add to your collection. This is a very nice village."* Keyworth post office has been run by the Soar/Eggleston family since 1944 and is still an important sorting office, employing 22 postmen and women.

32. As in many villages, the post office at **Kingston on Soar** has had a number of locations. From 1949-52, Bessie Gibbins ran the post office at 9 The Green, the cottage to the left of this row. This postcard, however, dates from the period 1952-58 when Evelyn Gibbins was sub postmistress at 7 The Green - the cottage to the right of the row.

Copyright
Knsl. 1.
The Post Office, Kneesall.
Raphael Tuck & Sons Ltd
London

33. Kneesall, like a number of Nottinghamshire villages today, now has no post office of its own. During the period 1925-54, Fortune House on Main Street served this purpose, with Raynor Heald acting as sub postmaster.

34. The Old Smithy on Collingham Road, **Langford**, had already served as the village post office from 1885-1901. When Sarah Ann Walker became sub postmistress in 1908, she used the same building. This postcard, written in Langford, has a Newark postmark from 1909.

35. A traction engine travels up **Lowdham** Main Street towards the building where, from 1892-1908, Mary Elizabeth Knight ran the village post office. The picture was taken by the prolific photographer and postcard publisher JH Scott, who was based in the nearby village of Bulcote.

36. A postcard published between 1959-65 by Landscape View Publishers of Market Harborough showing the post office in the village of **Mattersey**, six miles north of Retford.

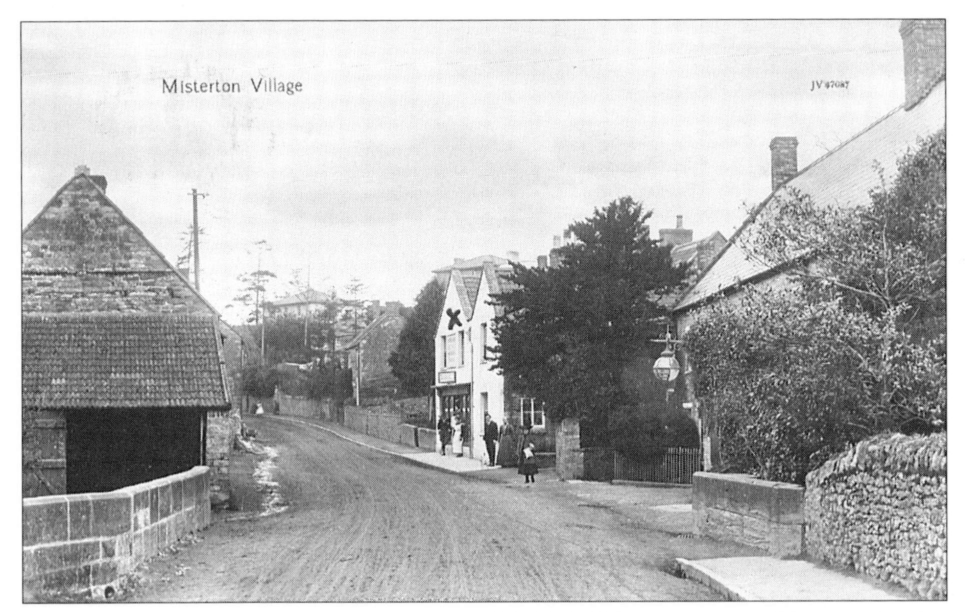

37. At the time this postcard was posted (1917), **Misterton** post office received its mail at 7.35am and 1.35pm from Gainsborough, five miles away. When John Wilson, a shoemaker, took on the role of sub postmaster in 1855, he began a family tradition, for the Wilsons ran Misterton post office for the next 143 years.

38. From 1916-37, the post office in the picturesque village of **Normanton on Soar** was based in this Tudor-style cottage at 73 Village Street. Letters arrived via Loughborough some three miles away. Card in the 'Plough' series.

39. A postcard sent from **Newark** four years after the new post office was built on Kirkgate in 1908. Local architects Saunders and Saunders were responsible for the design of the building, which was constructed by George Brown and Company. At the end of the 1990s, postal business was transferred to a local Co-op shop, and this building has been converted into a themed pub.

40. Two bicycles, a motor cycle and sidecar, and a pair of horses were captured on film by the Raphael Tuck and Sons photographer outside the post office on Low Street, **North Wheatley**. No date is indicated, although Mr Leatherland, whose name appears on the sign, was sub postmaster from 1921-57.

41. The impressive main post office building in **Nottingham** was constructed in 1898 at a cost of £95,000. The post office moved to premises at the top of Queen Street in 1972.

42. Sent from **Ollerton** on 1 January 1905, this postcard in the 'Dukeries' series shows the post office, which was run by Arthur Morris, along with a chemist's business from the same premises. The building dates from the Georgian period when it was built as a farmhouse. The shop was sold in the early years of this century, and the post office now operates from smaller premises round the corner.

PLACE, OLLERTON. NO·329

43. The village of **Plumtree**, five miles from Nottingham, had its own post office until quite recently. It was run from this building situated opposite *The Griffin* public house until the last postmistress, Mrs Joyce Richmond, retired in 1996. Now residents have to travel to nearby Tollerton or Keyworth to use a post office.

44. By 1921, the population of **Radcliffe on Trent** had risen to 1849. In the Directory of 1925, Fred Barrett is recorded as postmaster and the village had its own Telephone Exchange and Call Office on Bingham Road, with Miss Ida Copley the clerk in charge. Card in 'Rex' series, no. 440.

45. The car is parked outside the post office in the village of **Rampton**, seven miles from Retford. This building housed the post office from 1895-1985. Notice the variety of advertising signs on the side of the shop.

46. The post office in **Ranskill**, three miles from Bawtry, was run by Reuben Brown before being he was succeeded by Jemima Smithson. The plaque on the building indicates that this row of houses was known as Gladstone Terrace.

47. Rempstone, in the far south of the county, received its mail via Loughborough in neighbouring Leicestershire. From 1937-61, John Gaze, tobacconist, also acted as sub postmaster. The post office was in the building on the left-hand side of the road.

48. The famous Bamforth company of Holmfirth published this postcard of **Stanford** village. The post office of this small community, one mile from Loughborough, was situated in a humble terraced cottage at 7 Main Street (near right), where Annie Trigg was sub postmistress from 1899-1931.

49. A privately-produced postcard from the Edwardian era. The writing on the front indicates that the picture of the men clearing the snow from the front of **Sturton le Steeple** post office was taken on Boxing Day 1906. The postcard was sent from the village on 10 September the following year, when the writer comments *"another grand day on this picture but a little cooler."*

50. The caption on this postcard by Nottingham company C & AG Lewis describes this building as 'The Old Post Office, **Sutton in Ashfield**'. Situated on King Street/Market Place, it served the role from 1852-1927 before operations were moved to premises on Brook Street at the corner of Morven Avenue.

51. The postman stands proudly with his bike outside the post office in the village of **Walesby** near Tuxford. Could the lady standing behind the postman be Alice Martha Smith, who acted as the village sub postmistress for 40 years from 1910-1950?

52. Charles William Bayes carrried out the role of sub postmaster in **Walkeringham** from 1901-46 before passing on the position to his son Eric Raymond Bayes, who served for a further 32 years. Although the postcard is postmarked Misterton in 1960, it appears to date from much earlier.

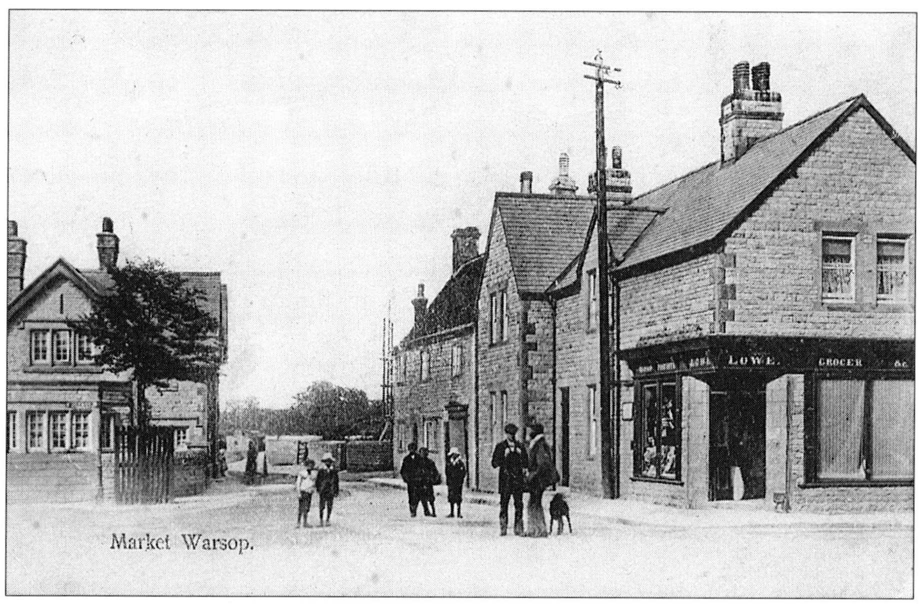

53. The shop on the corner of Burns Lane, **Warsop**, housed the village post office from 1881-1993. Charles Lowe, famer, grocer and tax collector, was sub postmaster for the first 27 years in these premises; a Mrs Fanny Lowe had the position from 1912-39.

54. The **Welbeck** Estate, ancestral home of the Dukes of Portland, was self-contained in many ways, having, for example, its own dairy and laundry. From the beginning of the twentieth century until the Second World War, it had its own post office run by the Hall family in Japonica Lodge. This postcard is postmarked Welbeck in May 1931.

55. The **Welbeck** Estate covered a large area of land with employees and their families living in various lodges and cottages. Here the postman on his delivery cart is handing over a letter outside one of the tunnel entrances.

56. West Bridgford, a large suburb of Nottingham, had a number of sub post offices. GF Heaney ran this one on Abbey Road. Like their country counterparts, the suburban shops tended to sell other goods as well as offering post office services. Note the two advertising signs for locally-produced Players cigarettes.

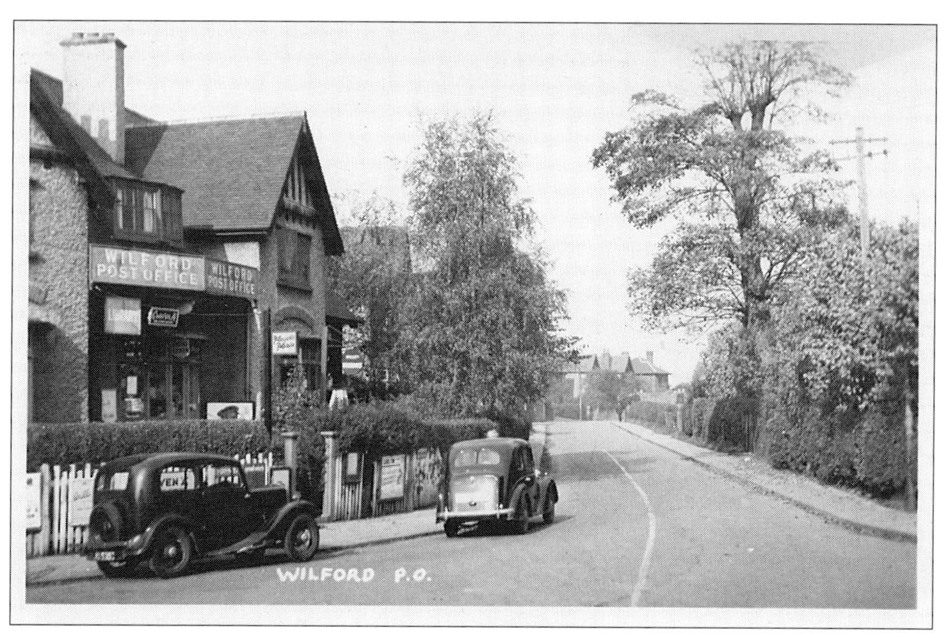

57. A pair of cars parked outside **Wilford** post office. An AW Bourne postcard, published in the 1950s. This shop was used as a post office from 1933-1997.

58. Wiseton Hall, the property of the Laycock family, dominated the village of **Wiseton**, one mile from Clayworth. Between 1899-1991, the post office was housed in this cottage close to the stable block.

59. Postally used in 1965, this postcard published by AW Bourne shows **Wollaton** post office situated in the village centre near the *Admiral Rodney* pub. At the time of this picture, Mr G Dunsmore was sub postmaster. The gardens to the front have won a number of prizes for their floral displays. Sadly, the post office closed in 2004.

60. The photographer has captured WP Henshaw's horse-drawn delivery vehicle from his 'Hygenic' bakery in Lambley as it stops outside **Woodborough** post office. The Foster family connection with the post office ran from John Foster's appointment as sub postmaster in 1881 to Charles P Foster's retirement in 1981. The card is postmarked 1916.

61. The tall building beyond the billiard hall in the foreground is **Worksop** post office. Built on Newcastle Avenue at a cost of £3,000, it opened in 1910, replacing one on Potter Street. Beyond it is the ornate facade of the Electric Theatre. Postcard published by R Sneath of Sheffield.

62. The single-storey building to the right served as **Wysall** post office from 1921-84. We can date the picture more accurately from the sign above the door: B Jeffrey, listed here as grocer and general dealer, was sub postmaster from 1937-42. The card was sent from Wymeswold Lane in the village to Sherwood, Nottingham, at a cost of 1d.

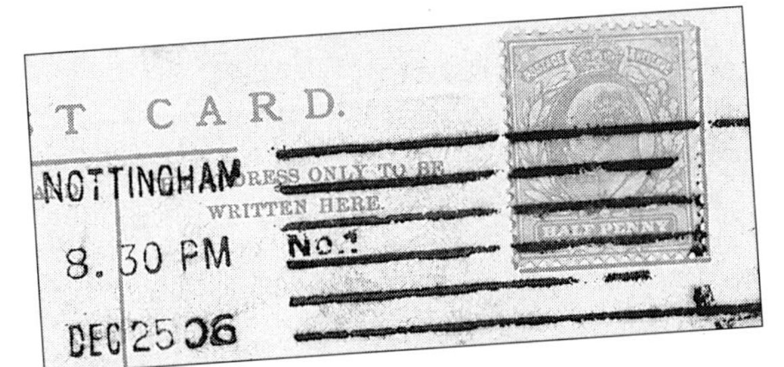

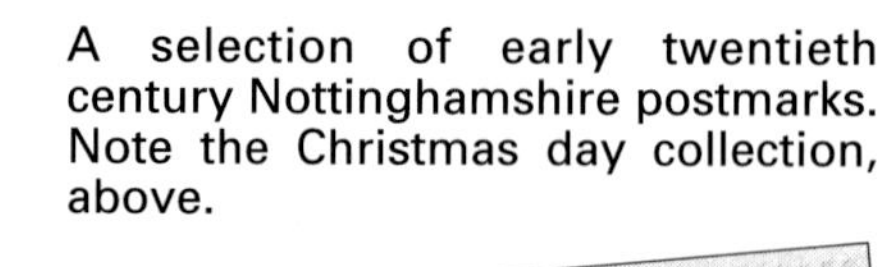
A selection of early twentieth century Nottinghamshire postmarks. Note the Christmas day collection, above.